SYLVIA EARLE

Extraordinary Explorer and Marine Biologist

by Rebecca Rowell

Content Consultant
Dr. Edward J. Buskey
Professor of Marine Science
University of Texas

Core Library

An Imprint of Abdo Publishing
abdopublishing.com

abdopublishing.com

Published by Abdo Publishing, a division of ABDO, PO Box 398166,
Minneapolis, Minnesota 55439. Copyright © 2016 by Abdo Consulting
Group, Inc. International copyrights reserved in all countries. No part of
this book may be reproduced in any form without written permission from
the publisher. Core Library™ is a trademark and logo of Abdo Publishing.

Printed in the United States of America, North Mankato, Minnesota
042015
092015

Cover Photo: Ben Rose/WireImage/Getty Images
Interior Photos: Ben Rose/WireImage/Getty Images, 1; John B. Carnett/
Bonnier Corp./Getty Images, 4; iStockphoto, 6, 9; AP Images, 10, 12,
22; Catala-Roca Digital Press Photos/Newscom, 14; Natali Snailcat/
Shutterstock Images, 19; Macduff Everton/National Geographic Creative,
20; OAR/National Undersea Research Program, 24, 43; Bettmann/
Corbis, 27; Roger Ressmeyer/Corbis, 30, 45; Bob Care/AP Images, 32;
Stockshoppe/Shutterstock Images, 34; Manuel Balce Ceneta/AP Images,
36; Stephen Frink/Corbis, 40

Editor: Jenna Gleisner
Series Designer: Becky Daum

Library of Congress Control Number: 2015931130

Cataloging-in-Publication Data
Rowell, Rebecca.
 Sylvia Earle: Extraordinary explorer and marine biologist / Rebecca Rowell.
   p. cm. -- (Great minds of science)
Includes bibliographical references and index.
ISBN 978-1-62403-874-7
1. Earle, Sylvia A., 1935- --Juvenile literature. 2. Women explorers--United
States--Biography--Juvenile literature. 3. Women marine biologists--United
States--Biography--Juvenile literature. I. Title.
578.77/092--dc23
[B]   2015931130

CHAPTER ONE

YOUNG EXPLORER

Sylvia Alice Earle was born in Gibbstown, New Jersey, on August 30, 1935. She grew up to become a pioneer in oceanography, the study of the ocean. She is known for exploring and researching the world's oceans. Earle knows the importance of oceans and the life forms that inhabit them. She also knows that oceans are needed for the survival of our planet and all of

Sylvia Earle has spent most of her life exploring the ocean.

As an advocate for the ocean, Earle works to protect the sea and its many inhabitants.

its life-forms, even the ones that live far from ocean waters. Through her dedicated work, Earle has become an ambassador for the ocean. She teaches the world about its amazing environment and inhabitants.

Discovering Her Love of the Ocean

Sylvia's interest in nature began when she was a young child. The second of three children, Sylvia grew up on a farm near Camden, New Jersey. As a young girl, she explored the woods by her home. She was always curious about the nature that surrounded her. Sylvia's family vacationed at the New Jersey shore during the summer. It was there that Sylvia developed a love of the ocean. She saw all kinds of interesting creatures on the edge of the Atlantic Ocean.

When Sylvia was 12 years old, she and her family moved to a very different environment.

Fascinating Finds

The wildlife Sylvia saw on the New Jersey shore fascinated her. It came in many shapes, colors, and sizes. And the creatures were active in different ways. She enjoyed watching the horseshoe crabs, their shiny brown bodies disappearing into the sand as they burrowed. Sandpipers, a type of bird, skipped on the water along the shore. She even observed tiny sand fleas—little creatures similar to shrimp and crabs—jumping around on seaweed.

Her family's new house was in Florida, on the Gulf of Mexico. She did not have to wait for summer vacation to enjoy the ocean. She could explore and play in it whenever she wanted. Sylvia investigated the beach just as she had wandered the woods in New Jersey. For Sylvia, her surroundings were a paradise. She saw many different life-forms—both animals and plants—and wanted to learn about all of them.

While living in Florida, Sylvia often saw dolphins. Sometimes dozens of them would swim near the shore by her house. She wanted to join them in the water. She liked how they swam quickly

Encouraged to Explore

Sylvia's mother, Alice, played an important role in helping Sylvia become a scientist. Alice encouraged her daughter to investigate and appreciate the world around her. She even encouraged Sylvia to get dirty and touch wild things. At least once, Alice brought a snake into the family's home. Alice helped young Sylvia understand its beauty and encouraged her to touch the snake, explaining to do so carefully because the animal was fragile.

As a young girl, Sylvia longed to swim like dolphins, free in the water.

and beautifully. Young Sylvia wanted to see well underwater, just like dolphins could, instead of feeling the sting of saltwater in her eyes. And she wanted to be able to breathe without having to lift her face out of the water.

Sylvia got her wish. She quickly learned she could see underwater by wearing a diving mask. It kept the

Sylvia Earle grew up to become an ocean explorer, expert, and advocate.

salty ocean water out of her eyes. Using a snorkel allowed her to breathe without lifting her head above water. With these pieces of equipment, she could observe underwater wildlife as never before.

FURTHER EVIDENCE

Chapter One discusses Sylvia Earle's childhood. Read the chapter again. What was Sylvia like as a child? What main idea, or ideas, does the chapter share about her early life? Many stories about Earle praise her work as a scientist. Does the evidence in this chapter support that idea? Read more about Earle at the website below. Find a quote about her childhood. Does the quote support the ideas in this chapter, or does it add new information?

Sylvia Earle's Life
mycorelibrary.com/sylvia-earle

CHAPTER TWO

BECOMING A SCIENTIST

Sylvia's passion for nature continued throughout her youth. Exploring the Gulf waters near her home made Sylvia want to know more about marine life. Knowledge about marine life was limited at the time. Sylvia decided to become a scientist and change that. She would discover the information herself.

Oftentimes the only woman on the crew, Earle proved herself capable of sea exploration and discovery.

Sylvia was a quick study. She often read the encyclopedia for fun. After graduating from high school in 1952 at the age of 16, she went to Saint Petersburg Junior College in Saint Petersburg, Florida. There she earned a degree in art at age 17.

In addition to her studies, Sylvia also learned how to scuba dive. In the early 1950s, when Sylvia was a teenager, scuba diving was fairly new. When Sylvia was 17 years old, she took advantage of an amazing opportunity. US Navy divers were stationed in Panama City, Florida. Sylvia went along on some of their research dives. She watched as they explored underwater.

Earle's First Dive

Earle still remembers her first scuba dive. After swallowing a bit of saltwater with her first breath, she got air. After a few breaths, she stopped thinking about breathing. It seemed to happen naturally. She turned her attention to a grunt, a little fish that was looking at her. Being underwater filled Sylvia with joy. She was like an underwater gymnast. She could flip and roll backward and forward. Sometimes she just hovered, mimicking the jellyfish she loved.

Ocean explorer and scientist Jacques Cousteau helped develop scuba diving in the 1940s.

By observing, she learned what she should and should not do as a scuba diver. Learning to scuba dive would shape Sylvia's future.

Studying Botany

Earle enrolled at Florida State University after earning her degree at Saint Petersburg. At Florida State her studies focused on botany, the study of plants. She graduated with a degree in 1955.

Earle kept studying botany, focusing on ocean plant life. In 1956 she earned an even higher degree in botany from Duke University in North Carolina. She continued working on a doctoral degree, the highest degree possible. While earning her degree at Duke University, she studied algae in the Gulf of Mexico. Earle used scuba diving to conduct her research. Some scientists were skeptical. These scientists thought people only scuba dived for fun, not science. Earle would prove these skeptics wrong.

Wife, Mother, and Researcher

Some scientists were skeptical for other reasons. One professor refused to allow Earle to be his teaching assistant because she was a woman. He thought she was going to get married, have children, and disregard her studies.

In 1957 Earle married scientist John Taylor. They had two children together. They later divorced, but becoming a mother did not keep Earle from exploring faraway locations. In 1964 Earle joined a six-week expedition to study the western Indian Ocean and beyond. She was the only

Defying Gender Roles

When Earle went on the expedition to the Indian Ocean in 1964, men dominated the sciences. Women who had gone on similar expeditions said they were often picked on. But Earle did not struggle with being the only woman on the ocean adventure. Her gender didn't bother her. She was serious about her mission and focused on her work.

woman on the research team, joining 70 men on the ocean adventure.

At that time, women were often thought of as inferior to men. Many men thought women belonged at home raising children, not sailing the seas, hauling heavy scuba tanks, and swimming with wild ocean creatures. They didn't think women were capable of the same skills or knowledge as men. Earle worked hard. She proved herself capable of conducting scientific work, including projects that required weeks at sea. She did all of this while also being a wife and a mother. Earle made news around the world. Her first expedition led to many more. Over the next two years, she joined expeditions to the Galápagos Islands, the Juan Fernandez Islands, and the Panama Canal Zone.

Algae Research

In 1966 Earle completed her doctoral studies. In 1967 she moved to Boston, Massachusetts. She worked at Harvard University and at the Radcliffe Institute

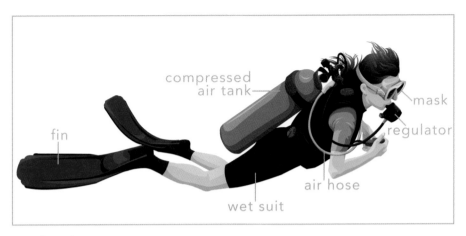

Scuba Gear

Sylvia Earle is an expert scuba diver. Her ability to scuba has helped her become an accomplished ocean researcher. She had to learn to use a variety of equipment, from a wet suit to an air tank with a collection of valves. Look closely at this diagram of scuba gear. How does seeing this diagram help you envision scuba diving and Earle's dives?

in Cambridge. Three years later Earle published her dissertation. This was her final report of her research for her doctoral degree. She titled it *Phaeophyta of the Eastern Gulf of Mexico. Phaeophyta* is the scientific name for brown algae. Using scuba, she had collected more than 20,000 samples of algae. This experiment was new because scuba diving was a new research tool. Until the 1950s, marine biologists collected algae samples that were washed ashore or pulled up with boat nets. This often meant the algae

Throughout her career, Earle has collected and studied algae, helping others learn more about it.

samples collected were damaged or dead and not in their original state.

Earle had carefully recorded the different types of brown algae she found and where she found them. The details she reported in her dissertation were brand-new information. Earle's research was so important that the top publication in her field, *Phycologia*, focused an entire issue on her dissertation. By the time Earle published her dissertation, she had spent more than 1,000 hours scuba diving. With that experience and her academic training, she was ready to make more history.

EXPLORE ONLINE

Chapter Two focuses on Earle's development as a scientist. It also touches on some of her experiences as a woman studying science. The website below also focuses on Earle. As you know, every source is different. How is the information given in the website different from the information in this chapter? What information is the same? How do the two sources present information differently? What can you learn from this website?

The Explorer: Sylvia Earle
mycorelibrary.com/sylvia-earle

CHAPTER THREE

A LEADER IN OCEANOGRAPHY

Earle continued to break ground as she built her career as an oceanographer. In 1970 she led an all-female crew. The two-week underwater mission was called Tektite II. She had applied to the first Tektite project in 1969 but was declined because she was a woman. She had more diving experience than anyone else who had applied. But the people who oversaw the project did

During the Tektite II project, Earle and her fellow female marine scientists spent up to 12 hours a day diving in the water.

Earle shows sea life samples to a fellow scientist during the Tektite II project.

not want men and women living together. The Tektite II team of five women spent the entire two weeks 50 feet (15 m) underwater. They lived and studied in the Tektite laboratory near Saint John Island, which is part of the Virgin Islands. The group studied the plants and fish in the area. They saw a variety of fish, including damselfish, parrot fish, surgeonfish, and wrasses. They recorded behavior, such as which fish arrived to a nearby reef early in the day and which visited later. They noticed that some fish were active during the day and slept at night, while others kept the opposite schedule. Earle observed that some fish even have favorite foods.

The team set a record. At the time, their study was the longest stretch of time below the ocean surface without interruption. The women's success made them celebrities. Tektite II was

Speaking Out

The Tektite II expedition changed Earle's life. The media and public treated Earle and her team members like celebrities. A parade was held in Chicago, Illinois, to honor them. At the event, without much notice, Earle was asked to give a speech. Radio and television stations relayed her words to the world. She knew that she represented herself, her team, women scientists—all scientists—and even the ocean to the millions of people listening and watching. She used everyday language so people who were not familiar with oceanography would understand. The speech was her first to a crowd. She succeeded. Public speaking soon became a regular part of Earle's life.

the first of more than 100 expeditions Earle would lead.

Discovering a New Plant

In 1975 Earle made history again. She made an important discovery while on an expedition on the submarine *Johnson Sea Link*. Earle was on the edge of a cliff in the waters of the Bahamas when she saw a gathering of plants. The grouping looked like a tiny forest. It was a type of seaweed that had never been documented. Earle got to officially name the plant because she discovered it. She called it *Johnson-sea-linkia profunda*, honoring the submarine used in the experiment. The word *profunda* in the name means "deep," indicating that the plant was found deep in the ocean.

Setting a World Record

In 1979 Earle set a world record. She had dreamed of diving deep, but it was not easy with scuba equipment. Scuba divers rely on air tanks to

Earle, wearing a Jim suit, prepares to descend to the ocean floor in 1979.

breathe underwater. But the gases in air tanks—oxygen and nitrogen—can become harmful under pressure. Pressure increases as divers venture deeper underwater. Because pressure increases with depth, divers can spend less time at deeper depths.

Earle found a way to dive deeper and stay longer at those depths. She used Jim, a special diving suit created in 1971. Jim suits are pressurized. Wearing it allows a diver to reach depths of 1,900 feet (580 m).

Studying and Saving Whales

In the 1970s Earle spent a lot of time with humpback whales. She studied them in the United States and beyond, traveling to Alaska and Hawaii, Bermuda, New Zealand, and South Africa. She viewed them from boats and while diving. She recorded the squeaks and groans of their language. Earle learned that hunting had caused whale numbers to drop—very low for some species. Earle realized she had to help protect whales. She promised to do what she could. That meant educating people about whales and the importance of protecting their home, the ocean.

A Jim diving suit looks similar to a space suit. The bulky suit weighed 1,000 pounds (454 kg). Earle spent weeks practicing using Jim. She learned how to get in and out of the suit, including its massive helmet. She learned how to move while in it.

Earle could not swim wearing Jim, so she needed help diving. On September 19, 1979, near Oahu, Hawaii, she rode deeper and deeper into the Pacific Ocean. She was strapped to the front of *Star II*, a small submarine. The submarine landed on the ocean floor 1,250 feet (381 m) below the water's surface. The strap holding her to *Star II* released. Earle walked on the ocean floor alone, unattached to the craft. She set a world record for the deepest untethered dive.

Deep Rover

Earle's dive in the Jim suit got her thinking about diving even deeper. She teamed with engineer and third husband Graham Hawkes to create an underwater craft. They talked about its shape and decided a sphere would be best. They considered glass and different metals. They even talked about lights. Earle would need them to see in the deep, dark water. Most important of all, they talked about the issue of air in the craft.

Earle and Hawkes formed the company Deep Ocean Engineering to build submarines. After four years of hard work, *Deep Rover* became reality. The submersible was round, and it operated without being tied to another craft. It was big enough for just one

Earle and Hawkes worked together to design Deep Rover.

person. In June 1984 Earle piloted the *Deep Rover* 3,000 feet (914 m) down into Pacific waters near San Diego, California. She did not reach the ocean's greatest depths, but she achieved her dream of going deeper into the waters she loved. And she advanced underwater technology in the process.

During her excursion in *Deep Rover* in June 1984, Earle saw more than wildlife. She described the experience in her autobiography, *Dive! My Adventures in the Deep Frontier*:

> *I could see tiny jellies, small shrimp, the glint of silver from a curious fish, and the translucent form of a speckled octopus. . . . As I neared maximum depth . . . something on the bottom seemed to flash in the sub's lights. . . . Cautiously, I moved closer. . . . I held my breath. . . . Suddenly I knew what it was. A soda can!*
>
> *It was not really a surprise. Whatever gets tossed into the sea doesn't just go away; it settles down in some other place, out of sight but not really gone.*

Source: Sylvia A. Earle. Dive! My Adventures in the Deep Frontier. *Washington, DC: National Geographic Society, 1999. Print. 9.*

Back It Up

In this passage, Earle uses evidence to support a point. Write a paragraph describing the point Earle is making. Then write down two or three pieces of evidence she uses to make her point.

CHAPTER FOUR

OCEAN EXPERT AND ADVOCATE

Earle has always strived to learn all she can about ocean life. She has also made sharing that knowledge a goal. She wants to educate people about the wonders of the ocean and its importance to the entire planet. In her effort to save the ocean, she stresses its importance in our survival, such as the crucial roles the ocean waters play in the water cycle.

Earle, left, takes a fish count to document fish population in the Florida Keys National Marine Sanctuary in 1997.

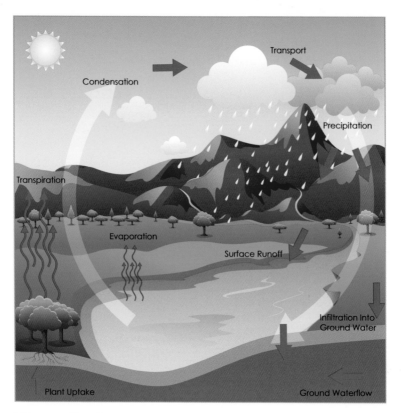

The Water Cycle

Earle advocates for the ocean because of its importance to life on Earth. Ocean water is at the heart of the water cycle that keeps water moving around the planet. This process causes water to become clouds that release rain and snow. Rain and snow fill lakes and rivers, sink into the ground, and flow back to the sea. From there, the process begins again. Along the way, the water gives life. Take a closer look at this diagram of the water cycle. How does seeing this diagram help you understand Earle's advocacy for protecting the planet's oceans?

Important Roles

As an ocean expert, Earle's knowledge has served

her in many jobs. During her career, she has worked

with a variety of organizations. In 1990 Earle became the first woman to serve as chief scientist for the National Ocean and Atmospheric Administration (NOAA). This government agency focuses on science, including watching the oceans, weather, coasts, and climate and teaching the public about them. In 1998 the National Geographic Society named Earle its first female explorer in residence. Through its Explorers in Residence Program, the society supports the work of top researchers around the world.

Writing and Speaking about the Ocean

In addition to researching the oceans, Earle writes about them. She has published more than 100 scientific papers. These papers help others understand her research findings. For example, Earle wrote about coral in Veracruz, Mexico, in 2004. And in 2009, she wrote about dangers to marine life in the Galápagos Islands.

Earle has traveled to more than 80 countries to give talks about the ocean and its importance to all life.

Earle has also written several books. Some are for young readers, such as her 1999 autobiography *Dive! My Adventures in the Deep Frontier*. All of her books teach about the ocean and its creatures. In her 2014 book *Blue Hope: Exploring and Caring for Earth's Magnificent Ocean*, Earle expresses her dream to save the ocean. In the book, she teaches about marine life, shares some of her own stories, and stresses to readers why everyone must care for the ocean. The book includes inspirational quotes, maps, and dozens of colorful photographs from above and below the water's surface.

Earle also speaks out for environmental preservation in radio and television interviews. Her goal is to help everyone—males and females, young and old, politicians and private citizens— understand that what humans do and do not do will affect the planet and all life on Earth.

Honored

Organizations around the world have recognized Earle's work as a scientist and as an environmentalist. She has received more than 100 awards. Some of the institutions have a female focus, such as the National Women's Hall of Fame

Awards and Recognition

Earle has earned many awards for her accomplishments. In 2014 *Glamour* magazine named Earle a Woman of the Year. Earle has earned some nicknames that acknowledge her work. *The New Yorker* magazine and the *New York Times* newspaper have called Earle "Her Deepness." *Time* magazine proclaimed her its first "Hero for the Planet." The US Library of Congress said she is a "Living Legend." And the United Nations Environment Programme decreed Earle a "Champion of the Earth."

and the Society of Women Geographers. Others focus on the environment. In 2014 the United Nations Environment Programme named Earle a "Champion of the Earth" and presented her with a lifetime achievement award.

Mission Blue

In 2009 Earle received an important award. Technology, Entertainment, Design (TED), an organization that promotes technology, education, and design, gave her $1 million to pursue her dream of saving the ocean. TED also held an event in 2010 to help Earle let others know about her goal. People donated more than $17 million to care for the oceans and to help Earle form Mission Blue. Through her organization, Earle aims to bring people and resources together to make 20 percent of the world's oceans protected areas. This means these areas would be safe from the effects of humans, such as limiting the amount of fishing. Some sites, such as those in the National Marine Sanctuary System, serve as places of learning, providing people with opportunities to experience ocean life and learn more about it. Currently less than 3 percent of ocean areas are protected. As of 2014, Earle had helped identify 51 hope spots. These are ocean areas she hopes to protect.

Continuing to Learn and Teach

Now in her 80s, Earle is as passionate as ever about ocean life. She spends approximately 300 days a year traveling in support of the ocean world she loves. And she continues to enjoy diving. Earle has logged more than 7,000 hours diving. She plans to dive as long as she is breathing.

National Parks in the Sea

One of Earle's ocean causes is National Marine Sanctuaries. These water areas are similar to underwater national parks. The US government preserves these sites because they are important as a resource. The United States has 13 of these sanctuaries, which include more than 180,000 square miles (466,000 sq km) of water. Earle serves as an advisor to the National Marine Sanctuary Foundation.

Earle swims alongside a submersible while assisting in oceanic research.

Sylvia Earle has played, studied, and lived in the ocean. In the process, she has advanced the fields of botany and oceanography and underwater exploration technology. More than a scientist, she has been a teacher. She has shared her understanding of ocean life with young and old alike, striving to also fight for the precious oceans the world needs. Earle has shown she has a great mind and a determined spirit. She also has a big heart, with a depth matched only by the ocean she readily returns to time and again.

In the beginning of her autobiography *Dive! My Adventure in the Deep Frontier*, Earle shares an inspiring note to her readers:

> If you want to be the first to go where no one has ever been before, you can. If you want to discover new kinds of animals, new plants, and whole new systems of life, they are there, deep in the sea. You can be the first to explore any of thousands of undersea mountains and cross unknown plains. . . .
>
> You can also dream up ways to explore the sea—with submersibles, underwater laboratories, robots, new sensors, cameras, and other instruments. If you want to, you can even build your own. I know such things are possible because I have had the fun of doing them and have glimpsed how much more there is to discover.

Source: Sylvia A. Earle. Dive! My Adventures in the Deep Frontier. *Washington, DC: National Geographic Society, 1999. Print. 7.*

What's the Big Idea?

What is the main point of the text? What does Earle want readers to learn from her experiences? What evidence does she give to support her idea?

Scuba for Science

Earle was one of the first marine scientists to use scuba diving for research. The technology was new at the time, and some scientists were skeptical, believing it was too fun to be useful to science. Using the underwater technology allowed Earle to explore ocean life near and far. Today scuba diving is commonplace in oceanography.

Landmark Research

Earle's dissertation research broke ground because she gathered new scientific information. Her collection and categorization of more than 20,000 samples of brown algae in the Gulf of Mexico showed the plant's variety and where it lives in that area. Her dissertation is so important that the Smithsonian is preserving it. Earle is a pioneer as a woman scientist. Her work includes discovering a species of algae and finding underwater land formations.

Deep Rover

Earle's collaboration with Graham Hawkes on the *Deep Rover* advanced the technology of submersibles. The submersible helps scientists explore the ocean at greater depths and with greater clarity than scuba or a Jim suit.

Ocean Awareness

Through speaking and writing, Earle has spread the word about the importance of ocean waters and wildlife and the role humans play in damaging and preserving them.

Say What?

Learning about oceanography can mean learning a lot of new vocabulary. Find five words in this book that you have never seen or heard before. Use a dictionary to find out what they mean. Then write the meanings in your own words, and use each word in a new sentence.

Surprise Me

Chapter Two discusses Earle's experiences becoming a scientist. After reading this book, what two or three facts about her life in science did you find most surprising? Write a few sentences about each fact. Why did you find each fact surprising?

Take a Stand

This book discusses the work of Sylvia Earle. Do you agree with her that humans need to take better care of the ocean? Write a brief essay explaining your opinion. Be sure to give reasons for your point of view. Include facts and details to support your reasons.

Why Do I Care?

Earle has spent her life fascinated by the ocean. She lives to learn about it and care for it. You may not live near the ocean. Perhaps you have never even seen it. How does the ocean affect your life? How does the ocean affect the world?

GLOSSARY

advocate
to support a cause; someone who supports a cause

algae
a plant or plantlike life-form, such as seaweed, that usually grows in water

ambassador
a representative; someone who speaks on behalf of another person or a thing

dissertation
a long piece of writing about a specific topic that usually involves extensive study and original research or thinking completed as part of earning a doctoral degree

expedition
a voyage or trip

oceanography
the science that studies oceans

skeptical
having doubt in something

submersible
a small craft designed to safely carry people underwater, especially to conduct research

untethered
to be free from; not tied to

LEARN MORE

Books

Earle, Sylvia A. *Blue Hope: Exploring and Caring for Earth's Magnificent Ocean.* Washington, DC: National Geographic, 2014.

Nivola, Claire A. *Life in the Ocean: The Story of Oceanographer Sylvia Earle.* New York: Frances Foster Books, Farrar Straus Giroux, 2012.

Websites

To learn more about Great Minds of Science, visit **booklinks.abdopublishing.com**. These links are routinely monitored and updated to provide the most current information available.

Visit **mycorelibrary.com** for free additional tools for teachers and students.

INDEX

ABOUT THE AUTHOR

Rebecca Rowell has put her degree in publishing and writing to work as an editor and an author of many books. Some of these topics as author include ancient India and the US Marine Corps. She lives in Minneapolis, Minnesota.